OF THE CROSS

According to the method of

St. Francis of Assisi

From the text published by
Msgr. M. A. Schumacher, M.A.

Arranged for Congregational Prayer

TAN Books
Charlotte, North Carolina

Nihil Obstat: Rt. Rev. Msgr. C. F. Conley
                  Censor Librorum Deputatus

Imprimatur: ✠ E. F. Hoban, D.D.
                  Bishop of Rockford, Illinois
                  March 21, 1939

The text for this edition of the Franciscan *Way of the Cross* was taken from *The Congregation Prays* by Rt. Rev. Msgr. M. A. Schumacher, M.A. The *Stabat Mater* and its English translation are from Fr. Lasance's *Blessed Sacrament Book* (Benziger Brothers, 1913), Imprimatur by John Cardinal Farley in 1913. The pictures are taken from *The Way of the Cross according to the Method of St. Alphonsus Liguori* published in 1908 by Benziger Brothers, New York, Cincinnati and Chicago.

ISBN: 978-0-89555-314-0

Printed and bound in the India

TAN Books
Charlotte, North Carolina
www.TANBooks.com
2012

The Stations of the Cross

According to the Method of
St. Francis of Assisi

PREPARATORY PRAYER

Together: O most merciful Jesus, * with a contrite heart and penitent spirit, * I bow down in profound humility before Thy divine majesty. * I adore Thee as my supreme Lord and Master; * I believe in Thee, * I hope in Thee, * I love Thee above all things. * I am heartily sorry for having offended Thee, * my Supreme and Only Good. * I resolve to amend my life, * and although I am unworthy to obtain mercy, * yet the sight of Thy holy cross, * on which Thou didst die, * inspires me with hope and consolation. * I will, therefore, meditate on Thy sufferings * and visit the stations of Thy Passion * in company with Thy sorrowful Mother and my guardian angel, * with the intention of promoting Thy honor * and saving my soul.

I desire to gain all the indulgences granted for this holy exercise * for myself and for the Poor Souls in Purgatory. * O merciful Redeemer, who hast said, * "And I, if I be lifted from earth, * will draw all things to Myself," * draw my heart and my love to Thee, * that I may perform this devotion as perfectly as possible, * and that I may live * and die in union with Thee. *Amen.*

3

First Station

JESUS IS CONDEMNED TO DEATH.

Stabat Mater dolorosa,
Juxta crucem lacrymosa,
Dum pendebat Filius.

FIRST STATION

Jesus is condemned to Death.

V. We adore Thee, O Christ, and we praise Thee,
R. Because by Thy holy cross Thou hast redeemed the world.

Priest: Jesus, most innocent, who neither did nor could commit a sin, was condemned to death, and moreover, to the most ignominious death of the cross. To remain a friend of Caesar, Pilate delivered Him into the hands of His enemies. A fearful crime—to condemn Innocence to death, and to offend God in order not to displease men!

People: O innocent Jesus, * having sinned, I am guilty of eternal death, * but Thou willingly dost accept the unjust sentence of death, * that I might live. * For whom, then, shall I henceforth live, * if not for Thee, my Lord? * Should I desire to please men, * I could not be Thy servant. * Let me, therefore, rather displease men and all the world, * than not please Thee, O Jesus.

Our Father. Hail Mary. Glory Be.

V. Lord Jesus, crucified,
R. Have mercy on us!*

> At the cross her station keeping,
> Stood the mournful Mother weeping,
> Close to Jesus to the last.

Second Station

JESUS IS MADE TO CARRY HIS CROSS.

Cujus animam gementem,
Contristatam et dolentem,
Pertransivit gladius.

SECOND STATION

Jesus is made to carry His Cross.

V. We adore Thee, O Christ, and we praise Thee,
R. Because by Thy holy cross Thou hast redeemed the world.

Priest: When our divine Saviour beheld the cross, He most willingly stretched out His bleeding arms, lovingly embraced it, and tenderly kissed it, and placing it on His bruised shoulders, He, although almost exhausted, joyfully carried it.

People: O my Jesus, * I cannot be Thy friend and follower, * if I refuse to carry the cross. * O dearly beloved cross! I embrace thee, I kiss thee, * I joyfully accept thee from the hands of my God. * Far be it from me to glory in anything, * save in the cross of my Lord and Redeemer. * By it the world shall be crucified to me * and I to the world, * that I may be Thine forever.

Our Father. Hail Mary. Glory Be.

V. Lord Jesus, crucified,
R. Have mercy on us!

> Through her heart, His sorrow sharing,
> All His bitter anguish bearing,
> Now at length the sword has passed.

Third Station

JESUS FALLS THE FIRST TIME.

O quam tristis et afflicta
Fuit ilia benedicta
Mater Unigeniti!

THIRD STATION

Jesus falls the First Time.

V. We adore Thee, O Christ, and we praise Thee,
R. Because by Thy holy cross Thou hast redeemed the world.

Priest: Our dear Saviour, carrying the cross, was so weakened by its heavy weight as to fall exhausted to the ground. Our sins and misdeeds were the heavy burden which oppressed Him: the cross was to Him light and sweet, but our sins were galling and insupportable.

People: O my Jesus, * Thou didst bear my burden and the heavy weight of my sins. * Should I, then, not bear in union with Thee, * my easy burden of suffering * and accept the sweet yoke of Thy commandments? * Thy yoke is sweet and Thy burden is light: * I therefore willingly accept it. * I will take up my cross and follow Thee.

Our Father. Hail Mary. Glory Be.

V. Lord Jesus, crucified,
R. Have mercy on us!

> Oh, how sad and sore distressed
> Was that Mother highly blessed
> Of the sole-begotten One!

Fourth Station

JESUS MEETS HIS SORROWFUL MOTHER.

Quae moerebat, et dolebat,
Pia Mater dum videbat
Nati poenas inclyti.

FOURTH STATION

Jesus meets his Sorrowful Mother.

V. We adore Thee, O Christ, and we praise Thee,
R. Because by Thy holy cross Thou hast redeemed
the world.

Priest: How painful and how sad it must have
been for Mary, the sorrowful Mother, to behold her
beloved Son, laden with the burden of the cross!
What unspeakable pangs her most tender heart expe-
rienced! How earnestly did she desire to die in place
of Jesus, or at least with Him! Implore this sorrowful Mother that she assist you in the hour of
your death.

People: O Jesus, O Mary, * I am the cause of the
great and manifold pains * which pierce your lov-
ing hearts! * Oh, that also my heart would feel and
experience * at least some of your sufferings! * O
Mother of Sorrows, * let me participate in the sufferings * which thou and Thy Son endured for me,
* and let me experience thy sorrow, * that afflicted
with thee, * I may enjoy thy assistance * in the hour
of my death.

Our Father. Hail Mary. Glory Be.

V. Lord Jesus, crucified,
R. Have mercy on us!

> Christ above in torment hangs,
> She beneath beholds the pangs
> Of her dying, glorious Son.

Fifth Station

SIMON OF CYRENE HELPS JESUS TO CARRY HIS CROSS.

Quis est homo qui non fleret
Matrem Christi si videret
In tanto supplicio?

FIFTH STATION

Simon of Cyrene helps Jesus to carry His Cross.

V. We adore Thee, O Christ, and we praise Thee,
R. Because by Thy holy cross Thou hast redeemed the world.

Priest: Simon of Cyrene was compelled to help Jesus carry His cross, and Jesus accepted his assistance. How willingly would He also permit you to carry the cross: He calls, but you hear not; He invites you, but you decline. What a reproach, to bear the cross reluctantly!

People: O Jesus! * Whosoever does not take up his cross and follow Thee, * is not worthy of Thee. * Behold, I join Thee in the Way of Thy Cross; * I will be Thy assistant, * following Thy bloody footsteps, * that I may come to Thee in eternal life.

Our Father. Hail Mary. Glory Be.

V. Lord Jesus, crucified,
R. Have mercy on us!

> Is there one who would not weep
> Whelmed in miseries so deep
> Christ's dear Mother to behold?

Sixth Station

VERONICA WIPES THE FACE OF JESUS.

Quis non posset contristari,
Christi Matrem contemplari
Dolentem cum Filio?

SIXTH STATION

Veronica wipes the Face of Jesus.

V. We adore Thee, O Christ, and we praise Thee,

R. Because by Thy holy cross Thou hast redeemed the world.

Priest: Veronica, impelled by devotion and compassion, presents her veil to Jesus to wipe His disfigured face. And Jesus imprints on it His holy countenance: a great recompense for so small a service. What return do you make to your Saviour for His great and manifold benefits?

People: Most merciful Jesus! * What return shall I make for all the benefits Thou hast bestowed upon me? * Behold, I consecrate myself entirely to Thy service. * I offer and consecrate to Thee my heart: * imprint on it Thy sacred image, * never again to be effaced by sin.

Our Father. Hail Mary. Glory Be.

V. Lord Jesus, crucified,

R. Have mercy on us!

> Can the human heart refrain
> From partaking in her pain,
> In that Mother's pain untold?

Seventh Station

JESUS FALLS THE SECOND TIME.

Pro peccatis suae gentis,
Vidit Jesum in tormentis,
Et flagellis subditum.

SEVENTH STATION

Jesus Falls the Second Time.

V. We adore Thee, O Christ, and we praise Thee,
R. Because by Thy holy cross Thou hast redeemed the world.

Priest: The suffering Jesus, under the weight of His cross, again falls to the ground; but the cruel executioners do not permit Him to rest a moment. Pushing and striking Him, they urge Him onward. It is the frequent repetition of our sins which oppresses Jesus. Witnessing this, how can I continue to sin?

People: O Jesus, Son of David, * have mercy on me! * Offer me Thy helping hand, and aid me, * that I may not fall again into my former sins. * From this very moment, * I will earnestly strive to reform: * nevermore will I sin! * Thou, O sole support of the weak, * by Thy grace, without which I can do nothing, * strengthen me to carry out faithfully this my resolution.

Our Father. Hail Mary. Glory Be.

V. Lord Jesus, crucified,
R. Have mercy on us!

> Bruised derided, cursed, defiled,
> She beheld her tender child,
> All with bloody scourges rent.

Eighth Station

THE WOMEN OF JERUSALEM
WEEP OVER JESUS.

Vidit suum dulcem natum
Moriendo, desolatum,
Dum emisit spiritum.

EIGHTH STATION

The Women of Jerusalem weep over Jesus.

V. We adore Thee, O Christ, and we praise Thee,
R. Because by Thy holy cross Thou hast redeemed the world.

Priest: These devoted women, moved by compassion, weep over the suffering Saviour. But He turns to them, saying: "Weep not for Me, Who am innocent, but weep for yourselves and for your children." Weep thou also, for there is nothing more pleasing to Our Lord and nothing more profitable for thyself, than tears shed from contrition for thy sins.

People: O Jesus, Who shall give to my eyes a torrent of tears, * that day and night I may weep for my sins? * I beseech Thee, through Thy bitter and bloody tears, * to move my heart by Thy divine grace, * so that from my eyes tears may flow abundantly, * and that I may weep all my days over Thy sufferings, * and still more over their cause, my sins.

Our Father. Hail Mary. Glory Be.

V. Lord Jesus, crucified,
R. Have mercy on us!

> For the sins of His own nation
> Saw Him hang in desolation
> Till His spirit forth He sent.

19

Ninth Station

JESUS FALLS THE THIRD TIME.

Eia Mater, fons amoris,
Me sentire vim doloris.
Fac, ut tecum lugeam.

NINTH STATION

Jesus Falls the Third Time.

V. We adore Thee, O Christ, and we praise Thee,
R. Because by Thy holy cross Thou hast redeemed the world.

Priest: Jesus, arriving exhausted at the foot of Calvary, falls for the third time to the ground. His love for us, however, is not diminished, not extinguished. What a fearfully oppressive burden our sins must be to cause Jesus to fall so often! Had He, however, not taken them upon Himself, they would have plunged us into the abyss of Hell.

People: Most merciful Jesus, * I return Thee infinite thanks * for not permitting me to continue in sin * and to fall, as I have so often deserved, * into the depths of Hell. * Enkindle in me an earnest desire of amendment; * let me never again relapse, * but vouchsafe me the grace * to persevere in penance to the end of my life.

Our Father. Hail Mary. Glory Be.

V. Lord Jesus, crucified,
R. Have mercy on us!

> O thou Mother! fount of love,
> Touch my spirit from above.
> Make my heart with thine accord:

Tenth Station

JESUS IS STRIPPED OF HIS GARMENTS.

Fac, ut ardeat cor meum
In amando Christum Deum,
Ut sibi complaceam.

TENTH STATION

Jesus is stripped of His Garments.

V. We adore Thee, O Christ, and we praise Thee,
R. Because by Thy holy cross Thou hast redeemed the world.

Priest: When Our Saviour had arrived on Calvary, He was cruelly despoiled of His garments. How painful this must have been because they adhered to His wounded and torn body, and with them parts of His bloody skin were removed! All the wounds of Jesus are renewed. Jesus was despoiled of His garments that He might die possessed of nothing; how happy will I also die after laying aside my former self with all evil desires and sinful inclinations!

People: Induce me, O Jesus, * to lay aside my former self * and to be renewed according to Thy will and desire. * I will not spare myself, * however painful this should be for me: * despoiled of things temporal, * of my own will, I desire to die, * in order to live for Thee forever.

Our Father. Hail Mary. Glory Be.

V. Lord Jesus, crucified,
R. Have mercy on us!

> Make me feel as thou hast felt;
> Make my soul to glow and melt
> With the love of Christ, my Lord.

Eleventh Station

JESUS IS NAILED TO THE CROSS.

Sancta Mater istud ages,
Crucifixi fige plagas
Cordi meo valide.

ELEVENTH STATION

Jesus is nailed to the Cross.

V. We adore Thee, O Christ, and we praise Thee,
R. Because by Thy holy cross Thou hast redeemed the world.

Priest: Jesus, being stripped of His garments, was violently thrown upon the cross and His hands and feet nailed thereto. In such excruciating pains He remained silent, because it pleased His heavenly Father. He suffered patiently, because He suffered for me. How do I act in sufferings and in troubles? How fretful and impatient, how full of complaints I am!

People: O Jesus, gracious Lamb of God, * I renounce forever my impatience. * Crucify, O Lord, my flesh and its concupiscences; * scourge, scathe, and punish me in this world, * do but spare me in the next. * I commit my destiny to Thee, * resigning myself to Thy holy will: * may it be done in all things!

Our Father. Hail Mary. Glory Be.

V. Lord Jesus, crucified,
R. Have mercy on us!

> Holy Mother, pierce me through!
> In my heart each wound renew
> Of my Saviour crucified.

Twelfth Station

JESUS IS RAISED UPON THE
CROSS AND DIES.

Tui nati vulnerati,
Tam dignati pro me pati
Poenas mecum divide.

TWELFTH STATION

Jesus is raised upon the Cross and Dies.

V. We adore Thee, O Christ, and we praise Thee,
R. Because by Thy holy cross Thou hast redeemed the world.

Priest: Behold Jesus crucified! Behold His wounds, received for love of you! His whole appearance betokens love: His head is bent to kiss you; His arms are extended to embrace you; His Heart is open to receive you. O superabundance of love, Jesus, the Son of God, dies upon the cross, that man may live and be delivered from everlasting death!

People: O most amiable Jesus! * Who will grant me that I may die for Thee! * I will at least endeavor to die to the world. * How must I regard the world and its vanities, * when I behold Thee hanging on the cross, * covered with wounds? * O Jesus, receive me into Thy wounded Heart: * I belong entirely to Thee; * for Thee alone do I desire to live and to die.

Our Father. Hail Mary. Glory Be.

V. Lord Jesus, crucified,
R. Have mercy on us!

> Let me share with thee His pain,
> Who for all our sins was slain,
> Who for me in torments died.

Thirteenth Station

JESUS IS TAKEN DOWN FROM
THE CROSS AND PLACED IN
THE ARMS OF HIS MOTHER.

Fac me tecum pie flere,
Crucifixo condolere,
Donec ego vixero.

THIRTEENTH STATION

Jesus is taken down from the Cross and placed in the Arms of His Mother.

V. We adore Thee, O Christ, and we praise Thee,
R. Because by Thy holy cross Thou hast redeemed the world.

Priest: Jesus did not descend from the cross but remained on it until He died. And when taken down from it, He in death as in life, rested on the bosom of His divine Mother. Persevere in your resolutions of reform and do not part from the cross; he who persevereth to the end shall be saved. Consider, moreover, how pure the heart should be that receives the body and blood of Christ in the Adorable Sacrament of the Altar.

People: O Lord Jesus, * Thy lifeless body, mangled and lacerated, * found a worthy resting-place * on the bosom of Thy virgin Mother. * Have I not often compelled Thee to dwell in my heart, * full of sin and impurity as it was? * Create in me a new heart, * that I may worthily receive * Thy most sacred body in Holy Communion, * and that Thou mayest remain in me * and I in Thee for all eternity.

Our Father. Hail Mary. Glory Be.

V. Lord Jesus, crucified,
R. Have mercy on us!

> Let me mingle tears with thee,
> Mourning Him Who mourned for me,
> All the days that I may live.

Fourteenth Station
JESUS IS LAID IN THE SEPULCHRE.

Juxta crucem tecum stare,
Et me tibi sociare,
In planctu desidero.

FOURTEENTH STATION

Jesus is laid in the Sepulchre.

V. We adore Thee, O Christ, and we praise Thee,
R. Because by Thy holy cross Thou hast redeemed the world.

Priest: The body of Jesus is interred in a stranger's sepulchre. He who in this world had not whereupon to rest His head, would not even have a grave of His own, because He was not from this world. You, who are so attached to the world, henceforth despise it, that you may not perish with it.

People: O Jesus, Thou hast set me apart from the world; * what, then, shall I seek therein? * Thou hast created me for Heaven; * what, then, have I to do with the world? * Depart from me, deceitful world, with thy vanities! * Henceforth I will follow the Way of the Cross * traced out for me by my Redeemer, * and journey onward to my heavenly home, * there to dwell forever and ever.

Our Father. Hail Mary. Glory Be.

V. Lord Jesus, crucified,
R. Have mercy on us!

> By the cross with thee to stay,
> There with thee to weep and pray,
> Is all I ask of thee to give.

CONCLUDING PRAYER

Together: Almighty and eternal God, * merciful Father, * who hast given to the human race Thy beloved Son * as an example of humility, obedience, and patience, * to precede us on the way of life, bearing the cross: * Graciously grant us that we, inflamed by His infinite love, * may take up the sweet yoke of His Gospel * together with the mortification of the cross, * following Him as His true disciples, * so that we shall one day gloriously rise with Him * and joyfully hear the final sentence: * "Come, ye blessed of My Father, * and possess the kingdom which was prepared for you from the beginning," * where Thou reignest with the Son and the Holy Ghost, * and where we hope to reign with Thee, * world without end. *Amen.*

STABAT MATER
(Conclusion)

Virgo virginum praeclara,
Mihi jam non sis amara,
Fac me tecum plangere;

Fac, ut portem Christi mortem,
Passionis fac consortem,
Et plagas recolere.

Fac me plagis vulnerari,
Fac me cruce inebriari,
Et cruore Filii.

Flammis ne urar succensus
Per te, Virgo, sim defensus
In die judicii.

Christe, cum sit hinc exire,
Da per Matrem me venire
Ad palman victoriae

Quando corpus morietur,
Fac ut animae donetur
Paradisi gloria. Amen

V. Ora pro nobis, Virgo dolorosissima.

R. Ut digni efficiamur promissionibus Christi.

Virgin of all virgins best!
Listen to my fond request:
Let me share thy grief divine;

Let me, to my latest breath,
In my body bear the death
Of that dying Son of thine.

Wounded with His every wound,
Steep my soul till it hath swooned
In His very Blood away.

Be to me, O Virgin, nigh,
Lest in flames I burn and die,
In His awful Judgment Day.

Christ, when Thou shalt call me hence,
Be Thy Mother my defense,
Be Thy cross my victory.

While my body here decays,
May my soul Thy goodness praise,
Safe in paradise with Thee. Amen.

V. Pray for us, Virgin most sorrowful.

R. That we may be made worthy of the promises of Christ.

Oremus	*Let us pray*
Interveniat pro nobis, quaesumus, Domine Jesu Christe, nunc et in hora mortis nostrae, apud tuam clementiam, beata Virgo Maria Mater tua, cujus sacratissimam animam in hora tuae passionis doloris gladius pertransivit. Per te, Jesu Christe, salvator mundi, qui cum Patre et Spiritu Sancto vivis et regnas, per omnia saecula saeculorum. Amen.	Grant, we beseech Thee, O Lord Jesus Christ, that the most blessed Virgin Mary, Thy Mother, through whose most holy soul, in the hour of Thine own Passion, the sword of sorrow passed, may intercede for us before the throne of Thy mercy, now and at the hour of our death. Through Thee, Jesus Christ, Saviour of the world, Who livest and reignest with the Father and the Holy Ghost, now and forever. Amen.

HOW TO GAIN A PARTIAL OR PLENARY INDULGENCE

To gain a partial indulgence, a Catholic in good standing must simply perform the prescribed work—in this case make the Way of the Cross—in the state of grace (that is, free of having committed a mortal sin that remains unforgiven in Confession) and have at least a general intention of gaining indulgences. A partial indulgence can be acquired more than once a day, unless otherwise expressly indicated.

To gain a plenary indulgence, however, several additional factors must also be present. All together, they are the following:

1. *The person must be a Catholic, not excommunicated, and in the state of grace*, that is, free from mortal sin that has not been confessed and forgiven in the Sacrament of Penance.

2. *The recipient must go to Confession, receive Holy Com-*

munion, and say at least one Our Father and one Hail Mary for the intentions of the Sovereign Pontiff. These can all be done several days before or after performing the prescribed "work," in this case, making the Way of the Cross. But it is more fitting that the Communion and the prayers for the Pope's intentions be on the same day that the "work" is performed. A single Confession suffices for gaining several plenary indulgences, but sacramental Communion must be received and prayer for the intention of the Sovereign Pontiff must be recited for the gaining of *each* plenary indulgence.

3. *The recipient must be free from all attachment to sin, even venial sin.* Although a person might still sin, as we all do, or even be inclined to an habitual sin, such as using God's name in vain, yet so long as the *attachment* to the sin or the *desire* to commit it is *absent* from the person's soul, he or she would be considered "free from attachment to sin." (If this disposition is in any way less than perfect or if any of the prescribed three conditions are not fulfilled, the indulgence will be only partial.)

4. *Only one plenary indulgence may be gained per day.* But one can obtain the plenary indulgence "for the moment of death," even if another plenary indulgence had been acquired on the same day.

5. *The person must perform the prescribed work,* in this case, make the Way of the Cross—*with at least the general intention of gaining indulgences.* In making the Way of the Cross, the following norms apply:

a. The pious exercise must be made before stations of the Way of the Cross legitimately erected.

b. For the erection of the Way of the Cross, fourteen crosses are required, to which it is customary to add fourteen pictures or images, which represent the stations of Jerusalem.

35

c. Although according to the more common practice the pious exercise consists of fourteen pious readings to which some vocal prayers are added, yet nothing more is required than a pious meditation on the Passion and Death of the Lord, which need not be a particular consideration of the individual mysteries of the stations.

d. A movement from one station to the next is required, but if the pious exercise is made publicly and if it is not possible for all taking part to go in an orderly way from station to station, it suffices if at least the one conducting the exercise goes from station to station, the others remaining in their places.

e. Those who are "impeded" can gain the same indulgence if they spend at least a half hour in pious reading and meditation on the Passion and Death of Our Lord Jesus Christ.*

---

*The above was taken from the *Enchiridion of Indulgences—Norms and Grants*, authorized English Edition, translated by Fr. William T. Barry, C.SS.R., Catholic Book Publishing Co., New York, New York, from the Second Revised Edition of the *Enchiridion Indulgentiarum* issued by the Sacred Apostolic Penitentiary, 1968 and originally published by Libreria Editrice Vaticana, Vatican City, 1968.